FIGHTING TO SURVIVE
AIRPLANE CRASHES

TERRIFYING **TRUE** STORIES

By Sean McCollum

COMPASS POINT BOOKS
a capstone imprint

Compass Point Books are published by Capstone Press
1710 Roe Crest Drive, North Mankato, Minnesota 56003
www.capstonepub.com

Library of Congress Cataloging-in-Publication Data
Names: McCollum, Sean, author.
Title: Fighting to survive airplane crashes : terrifying true stories / by
  Sean McCollum.
Description: North Mankato, Minnesota : Compass Point Books, [2020] | Series:
  Fighting to survive | Includes bibliographical references and index. |
  Audience: Ages: 10 to 14.
Identifiers: LCCN 2019007145 | ISBN 9780756561833 (hardcover) | ISBN
  9780756562304 (pbk.) | ISBN 9780756562052 (eBook PDF)
Subjects: LCSH: Aircraft accidents—Juvenile literature. | Airplane crash
  survival—Juvenile literature.
Classification: LCC TL553.5 .M338 2020 | DDC 363.12/4—dc23
LC record available at https://lccn.loc.gov/2019007145

Editorial Credits
Kristen Mohn, editor; Terri Poburka, designer; Morgan Walters, media researcher; Kathy
McColley, production specialist

Photo Credits
Alamy: Photo 12, 6, ROUSSEL BERNARD, 5, WorldFoto, 9, ZUMA Press, Inc, 37, 58;
Associated Press: Ed Porter, 32, James Finley, 35, Jeff Bundy, 30, Steven Day, 57, The
Sioux City Journal, Dawn J. Sagert, 29, Trela Media, 55; Getty Images: Bettmann, 25, John
Warburton-Lee, 10, Portland Press Herald, 15, TONY KARUMBA, 45; Newscom: Delphine
Goldsztejn/ZUMA Press, 46, Gary Anderson/Sioux City Journal/ZUMAPRESS, 27, Reg
Innell/Toronto Star/ZUMA Press, 18, Reg Innell/ZUMA Press, 20, SMG/ZUMA Press,
49; Science Source: CLAUS LUNAU, 52; Shutterstock: ClickHere, (smoke) Cover, Enrico
Romiti, 38, IndianSummer, 23, Isaac Marzioli, (ink) design element throughout, Kamenetskiy
Konstantin, (plane) Cover, MaxyM, 4, Miloje, (grunge) design element throughout, pavalena,
13, Serban Bogdan, 40, xpixel, (paper) design element throughout; Wikimedia: Aleks B., 43,
Steve Fitzgerald, 17

Printed and bound in the USA.
PA71

TABLE OF
CONTENTS

INTRODUCTION

Getting on an aircraft for the first time can be a life-changing experience. This seemingly magical machine carries us tens of thousands of feet above Earth while we sit in a chair and read a magazine or watch a movie. It can transport us across the country or around the world in a matter of hours.

But it's not magic. It's science. And rules, regulations, and training make flying one of the safest forms of travel. Statistics prove flying in a plane is much safer than riding in a car. In 2016 there were more than 800 million air passengers in the United States. There were 108 accidents that killed 29 people. That same year more than 7 million car accidents were reported. They resulted in the deaths of 37,461 people.

Most plane crashes involve small, private planes, not commercial jets.

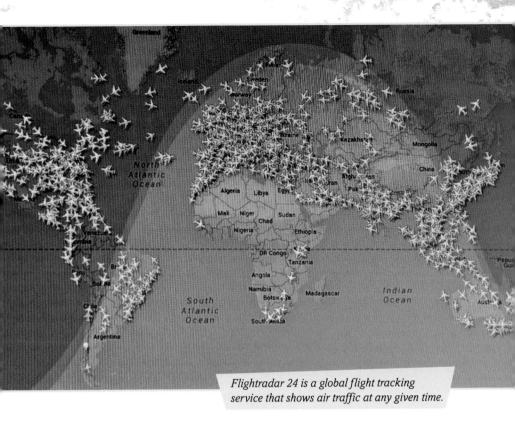

Flightradar 24 is a global flight tracking service that shows air traffic at any given time.

However, when an aircraft crashes or faces midair danger, it grabs the world's attention. It is terrifying to think of something going wrong so high above Earth. People on the ground worry about those in danger, demanding to know the details. People want to know what happened and how we can make sure it never happens again. And perhaps we wonder how we would react if we were on that plane. Would we cry out? Hold the hand of a stranger? Pray? If we are fortunate, we will never have to know.

Here are five breathtaking and heartrending aviation survival stories: four harrowing crashes and one teen stowaway. They highlight the experiences, courage, and heroism of people as they face the most terrifying moments of their lives—and hope to live to see another day.

LOST IN ALASKA
CESSNA 207 SKYWAGON

Alaska covers a vast territory of more than 660,000 square miles (1.7 million square kilometers), making it by far the largest state in the United States. Much of it is covered with roadless wilderness, including long mountain ranges, forests, and tundra. Alaska's great distances and limited roadways make air travel the most sensible means of transportation. Small aircraft provide vital links across the state. They connect the many remote villages that dot Alaska's backcountry, delivering mail, goods, and people.

A NEW LIFE IN A NEW PLACE

For Donald Evans, Alaska had been love at first sight. The Frontier State, as Alaska is known, charmed him on his first visit there in the early 2000s. After completing his service with the U.S. Marines in 2007, Evans made the move, along with his wife, Rosemarie, and their two children, Donnie and McKenzie. In 2011 Evans and Rosemarie were hired as a teaching team, splitting one position in the two-room grade school in Anvik, Alaska. Located

The Cessna 207 Skywagon, the type of plane Ernie Chase flew, can go 610 miles (982 km) before refueling.

about 225 miles (360 km) northwest of Anchorage, Anvik is a remote bush village of about 85 people.

That August the Evans family flew to McGrath, Alaska, for a week of teacher meetings. While there, Rosemarie learned she was pregnant with another child. She and Evans were excited about the news.

On August 13 they headed to the airport to return to Anvik with their children and fellow teacher, Julia Walker. At around 7:40 p.m. pilot Ernie Chase saw a break in the fog and cloud cover. He readied his six-seater Cessna 207 Skywagon for takeoff for the quick 148-mile (238-km) flight from McGrath to Anvik, a route he flew regularly. On board were all three of Anvik's grade school teachers along with two of its students—10-year-old Donnie and 8-year-old McKenzie. With the first day of classes only a week away, they were all excited to get back for final preparations.

Chase, 66, was a veteran bush pilot who flew out of his hometown of Anvik. Bush pilots are pilots who fly routes in sparsely settled areas, taking off and landing on rough landing strips or at small airports. Alaskan bush pilots like Chase are legendary for their daring and guts. Alaskan weather can change in a snap, which requires pilots to have good instincts, good judgment, and a healthy dose of good luck. But good luck can't be counted on.

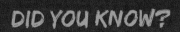

Clouds swallowed the single-engine plane as it gained altitude. Within 20 minutes, visibility was almost zero, a condition known as whiteout. Chase knew they might be in trouble. "This is pretty bad," Evans recalled Chase saying.

Chase decided to turn around and head back to McGrath to play it safe. He dropped altitude to see if he could fly below the cloud cover. He climbed again, then dropped again, apparently trying to get his bearings.

Evans was seated beside Chase. Suddenly the pilot banked hard to his right, as if he had seen what was coming. A hole opened in the clouds, and Evans saw a low mountain dead ahead. "Pull up!" he shouted at Chase. It was too late. The Cessna 207 crashed into a brown and green mountain slope that was covered in stunted trees.

FIGHTING TO SURVIVE

After the crash Evans was the first to regain consciousness. There was still daylight—in August the Alaskan sun does not set until after 10 p.m. It was raining heavily, though, and thick, low clouds hung over them. The impact had broken the Cessna 207 Skywagon in half.

One look told Evans that the pilot was dead. So was fellow teacher Walker, who had been seated directly behind Evans. As his head cleared, Evans began looking and listening for signs of

life from his family. Rosemarie was not moving, and he could not see his children in the far back of the plane. He listened for signs of life and at first heard nothing. He had the devastating thought that the crash had killed everyone but him.

Then he heard crying. It was McKenzie, somehow and somewhere outside the body of the plane. Ignoring his own pain, Evans freed himself from the wreckage and crawled out to find her. She had been thrown about 20 feet (6 meters) from the plane. Father and daughter pulled themselves back toward the aircraft. Drenched by the cold rain, McKenzie was shivering and at risk of hypothermia. One arm was broken, and she had other injuries as well.

Because Anvik is so remote and has so few people, it's ideal for the Iditarod Trail Sled Dog Race.

Evans helped McKenzie take off her cold, wet clothes and wrapped her in the yellow and pink quilt she had made during their week in McGrath. He later added layers of cardboard and plastic garbage bags to provide more insulation against the wet chill. As the sun sank lower, the temperature did too. It was in the low 50s and falling.

By this time his wife, Rosemarie, was coming to and experiencing terrible pain. She would later learn that she had broken her back, ankles, feet, and one arm. She was also trapped in the wreckage. Still, she tried to reach back with her good arm to find Donnie, who had been seated behind her.

Donnie had regained consciousness as well. He was screaming from the back of the plane. His legs and waist were trapped under the

The small town of Anvik, Alaska, has a population of fewer than 100 people.

plane's crumpled floorboards. To reach Donnie, his father climbed on top of the aircraft. Then he dropped through an opening and landed beside his son. He knew he had to get the pressure off Donnie's lower body. He tried using a willow tree branch as a lever to lift the debris off the boy. Then Evans remembered the pruning shears for trimming trees and bushes that he had in his gear. He found the scissors-like tool and used it to cut away the floorboards. Donnie was still in severe pain, but he was out of immediate danger.

Finally, Evans was able to help his wife. Rosemarie was spitting up blood and having trouble breathing. She drifted in and out of consciousness. Evans was able to shift some of the wreckage off her to relieve the pressure, but she was still trapped.

Evans, a war veteran, had been powered by adrenaline as he rushed to save his family. As his energy ebbed, though, he realized he was badly hurt himself. His jaw was broken and several teeth were missing. He also had fractures in his feet, legs, and back from the impact. They were all severely injured, but somehow the entire Evans family had survived. Yet Evans knew their ordeal was far from over.

They needed emergency help, but how would rescuers find them? Then Evans remembered—before takeoff he had seen a locator beacon attached to one of the cockpit's sun visors. Bush pilots carry these pocket-sized devices for such a misfortune. When activated, it bounces a distress signal off satellites, reporting its location to authorities. Evans found the beacon and activated it. Now they hoped someone would receive their desperate call for help.

At 8:30 p.m. the message was received. The crash site was only about 37 miles (60 km) from McGrath, but it was far from any road or trail. Other planes from the commuter service took off to begin a search. However, strong winds, clouds, and rain soon forced them to retreat. The Alaska Air National Guard had also been notified. This group is one of the most fearless and decorated rescue units in the world. Their motto: "These things we do, that others may live."

It was a race against time, and a battle against the elements.

SO CLOSE, SO FAR

Evans felt a surge of hope as he heard aircraft circling overhead some time later. However, he could not see their lights through the thick cloud cover. At 10:45 p.m. the sun went down. The family was scared, wet, cold, and in a great deal of pain. Now they were also in the dark.

Evans hoped at any moment they would hear the sound of a rescue helicopter chopping through the night. Instead, they heard the howling of wolves in the distance. The idea of wolves finding them trapped in the Alaskan wilderness was a terrifying thought. Donnie and McKenzie started screaming. Evans reassured his children to calm them down.

The minutes turned into hours, and all they could do was wait. The family prayed and sang together. Evans was determined to keep everyone awake. He feared that if any of them fell asleep or lost consciousness again, they would never wake up.

Meanwhile, rescuers continued searching for the lost plane. An Air National Guard HC-130 plane took off from Anchorage, more than 200 miles (320 km) away. This big prop plane is used by the U.S. military in search-and-rescue missions. It circled above the crash site at about 3 a.m. but could not see the downed Cessna. It was forced back to base to refuel. At 9 a.m. a National Guard HH-60 Pave Hawk helicopter took off, soon followed by the HC-130.

Anvik is about 148 miles (238 km) from McGrath.

Evans, Rosemarie, Donnie, and McKenzie were losing strength and hope. From the cargo area, Evans retrieved a bag of small oranges he had been bringing back to Anvik as a special treat. Now he passed out a piece of fruit to each of them. He knew they were in agony. He finally told them it was okay to go ahead and fall asleep if they needed to.

But within minutes of eating the oranges, they heard the helicopter again. Its crew had spotted the crash site through a break in the clouds. The time was a little after 11 a.m., more than 15 hours after the crash. The chopper could not land on the mountain slope, but a pair of pararescuers—known in Alaska as "Guardian Angels"—lowered themselves to the ground on cables.

Evans asked the rescuers to take Rosemarie first, since she was pregnant. They loaded her into a rescue basket, which was lifted to the helicopter. The crew flew her to McGrath, then returned to rescue the rest of the family. From McGrath, the Evanses were immediately airlifted to Anchorage, where they could get the best emergency treatment.

All four members of the Evans family endured months of recovery. McKenzie underwent surgery to treat her internal injuries. Donnie had to have surgery on his skull. Evans and Rosemarie spent months in wheelchairs as they healed from all their broken bones, including broken backs. Then, seven months after the crash, Rosemarie gave birth to a healthy baby girl—Willow Julia Grace Evans.

Investigation of the crash put the blame on the sudden change of weather. Chase had been flying by "visual flight rules" (VFR). VFR requires pilots to be able to navigate by sight. When the heavy clouds enveloped the plane, he lost his bearings, which led to the crash. Pilots—especially those flying in regions with weather as unpredictable as Alaska's—are urged to learn how to fly in "instrument meteorological conditions" (IMC). The ability to fly IMC means that pilots can use their instruments and sensors alone to determine their position, altitude, and speed to avoid danger, even in whiteout conditions.

The crash took the lives of Chase and Walker in an instant. The Evans family, though, had survived with the help of luck, courage, and determination. Their rescue was also a testament to the training and skills of the Alaska Air National Guard.

Two years after the accident, the Evans family, including baby Willow, recounted their story to a reporter.

DID YOU KNOW?

About 35 percent of air commuter crashes in the United States occur in Alaska, according to the National Institute for Occupational Safety and Health. All Alaskan pilots are required by law to carry a survival kit, and a distress beacon

THE STOWAWAY
IBERIA AIRLINES FLIGHT 904

The two boys hid in the tall grass at the end of the runway. It was late afternoon on June 3, 1969. They had been scouting aircraft at José Martí Airport in Havana, Cuba. Now they were ready to put their dangerous plan into action. The Iberia Airlines Flight 904 taxied toward them, its engines roaring. It made a turn, then paused on the runway while the flight crew conducted its final preflight checks. Next stop—Madrid, Spain, more than 4,600 miles (7,400 km) across the Atlantic Ocean.

For Armando Socarrás Ramírez, 17, and his friend Jorge Pérez Blanco, 16, it was now or never. They sprinted onto the runway toward the landing gear. They planned to climb inside the wheel wells where the gear was stowed during flight. Earlier, they had secretly scouted the compartments and believed they could fit. However, neither had ever been on an aircraft and had almost no understanding of what they were about to attempt.

The teens split up. Jorge clambered up the large double wheels and into the left wheel well. Armando did the same into the right compartment. Before Armando could get situated, the plane began rolling. He desperately grabbed on to anything he could reach. Though his ears were stuffed with cotton, the engine noise became earsplitting as the aircraft accelerated for takeoff. The runway below him turned into a high-speed blur. Then the wheels of the DC-8 jet left the ground. There was no turning back now.

The landing gear began to retract into the compartment. Armando's fear turned to panic as the large wheels closed in on him. He pressed himself against the wall, trying to make himself as skinny as possible. He and his hope for a new life outside of Cuba seemed inches away from being crushed.

ESCAPE FROM CUBA

Armando Socarrás Ramírez was born in Cuba, an island country about 100 miles (160 km) south of the tip of Florida. It was—and still is—a communist country. The government, then led by dictator Fidel Castro, controlled almost everything in Cuban society, including news, business, education, food, and social life. Citizens were not allowed to leave the country without the government's permission. Most Cubans were very poor, with few chances to work toward a better life. Armando lived in a one-room home with 10 other family members. Armando and Jorge saw Cuba as a kind of prison surrounded by the Caribbean Sea.

According to Armando, he and Jorge hoped to find more opportunities and freedom elsewhere. Armando's uncle had escaped Cuba two years earlier and was living in the United States.

Armando and Jorge attempted to stow away on a Douglas DC-8 jet.

The teen wanted to join him there. He wanted to be an artist. At 16, though, Armando had been sent to a job-training school to learn welding. He was also required to work in the sugarcane fields. Then he met Jorge, who shared his dream of escape and had an idea about how to make it happen.

At that time the United States had blocked almost all travel to and from Cuba. There was also an economic embargo that blocked or limited trade between Cuba and the United States. International airlines, including Iberia, maintained a limited number of flights

Communist leader Fidel Castro ruled Cuba for nearly five decades.

to Havana. Jorge knew about the weekly midafternoon flight from Havana to Madrid. There was no way they could afford a ticket, even in the unlikely event Cuban authorities gave them permission to leave the country. But was it possible to hide in a plane and fly to freedom? Twice the two boys visited the airport to watch Flight 904 as the passenger jet taxied on the runway and took off. From what they could tell, there seemed to be room in the wheel wells for them to stow away.

Now the jet rose toward cruising altitude. Armando had accomplished the first part of the plan by sneaking into the compartment. Surviving inside for the nearly eight-and-a-half-hour flight would prove even more difficult and dangerous.

AIRBORNE

As Flight 904 left the ground, the huge wheels of the landing gear retracted. Blistering hot from the friction of takeoff, they closed in on Armando and threatened to crush him. In desperation, he tried to push the wheels away with his feet. It was useless. The landing gear locked into place. The bay doors closed beneath him, blocking out all light.

Almost immediately, though, the doors reopened and the wheels lowered. Staring out into the open air, Armando feared he'd somehow been caught. He grabbed on to a pipe and held on as turbulence buffeted inside the wheel well. He was sure the aircraft was circling back to deliver Jorge and him to the police.

In reality, a red light had come on in the cockpit. It warned the pilot, Captain Valentin Vara del Rey, that the landing gear had not retracted properly. He followed procedure and lowered the wheels, then retracted them again. The warning light stopped flashing.

In those moments when the captain reset the landing gear, Armando was able to shift himself into a more secure position.

Now he swallowed aspirin to try to relieve the headache caused by the roaring engine noise. Using a rope he had brought, he made a halfhearted attempt to tie himself to some of the equipment inside the compartment. The hope was that it would keep him from falling out when the plane lowered its landing gear on the approach to Madrid.

The aircraft climbed to its cruising altitude of 29,000 feet (8,800 m). The passengers inside the aircraft were enjoying an in-flight meal. As

Castro gave many speeches in Revolution Square, Havana, where heroes of the revolution were honored.

with all high-altitude flights, the cabin was pressurized and sealed so people could breathe normally. Heating systems were set at a comfortable temperature compared to the subzero cold of the high-altitude air outside. People could sit back, relax, read, or nap.

Hidden below them, Armando was having a much different experience. He had no knowledge of the workings of commercial airliners. The wheel wells of passenger aircraft are not heated. Armando was soon colder than he knew was possible, enduring brutal temperatures less than minus 40° Fahrenheit (minus 40° Celsius). He was not prepared for such extreme cold. He wore only a shirt and pants with a light jacket. He had also lost a shoe when he climbed aboard.

Nor was the wheel well pressurized with oxygen-rich air. Armando was breathing the very thin air at that altitude—the same as at the peak of Mount Everest, where mountain climbers use oxygen tanks to breathe. The air at that altitude contains about 33 percent of the oxygen found at sea level. Armando found it harder and harder to think. He hoped Jorge was okay in the other wheel well. He thought about his family and friends back in Havana. He drifted in and out of consciousness. About two hours into the flight, he passed out.

DID YOU KNOW?

Between 1947 and 2015 the U.S. Federal Aviation Administration (FAA) counted 113 attempts to stow away in the wheel wells of aircraft. During those attempts, 86 people died.

"IMPOSSIBLE! IMPOSSIBLE!"

The sun was rising in Spain as Iberia Flight 904 began its approach to Madrid. It was about 8 a.m. local time. With other aircraft waiting to land, the jet went into a holding pattern, slowly losing altitude. Finally it was Flight 904's turn. It lowered its landing gear, causing the jet to shudder as the wheels created drag in the air. With the bay doors now open, high-speed wind blasted into the wheel wells.

A veteran pilot, Captain Vara del Rey made a smooth landing. The plane rolled to a stop, and the passengers deplaned. The crew did its normal postflight checks, then waited for transportation to ferry them to the airport terminal. Mechanics and other ground crew arrived to begin preparing the aircraft for its next flight.

They were shocked when a body dropped out of the wheel well. Somehow the unconscious Armando had stayed inside as the landing gear was lowered and wind gusts of more than 150 miles (240 km) per hour whipped into the compartment. His thin clothes were frozen stiff. Ice covered his nose and mouth, and his skin was pale. A member of the ground crew rushed up and heard the motionless figure moan. As rescue vehicles were called, Captain Vara del Rey hurried over. "Impossible! Impossible!" he kept saying.

Armando was rushed to a Madrid hospital. His body temperature was 93°F (34°C)—well below normal. Slowly, he regained consciousness, and hospital staff soaked his hands and feet in warm water to treat his frostbite. He recalled someone saying, "He is alive!" He asked if he had made it to Spain and was relieved when the answer was yes. He then inquired about Jorge, but no one knew anything about Armando's friend. To this day, what happened to Jorge Pérez Blanco is unknown. Perhaps he failed to climb into the compartment and was arrested in Cuba and disappeared into one of its prisons. Most people assume he fell from the wheel well at some point when the landing gear was lowered.

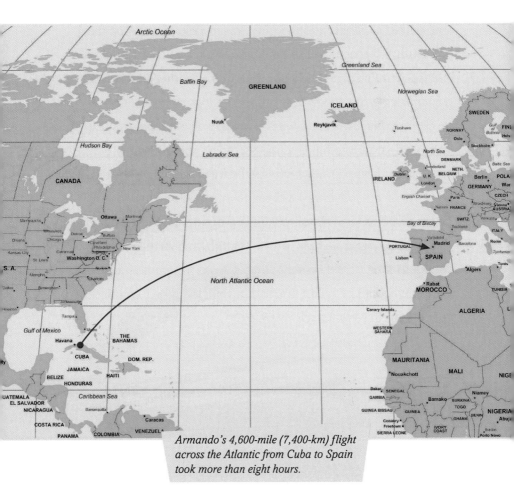

Armando's 4,600-mile (7,400-km) flight across the Atlantic from Cuba to Spain took more than eight hours.

FROZEN ALIVE

How did Armando Socarrás Ramírez survive his transatlantic ordeal? Doctors have called it nothing less than a miracle. He had frostbite but otherwise suffered little permanent harm. The dropping temperature in the wheel well gradually slowed Armando's body functions. It reduced his heart rate and the need for oxygen. In a sense, his body protected itself by going into a kind of hibernation. Some experts also speculated that the gradual descent of the holding pattern over Madrid also helped Armando. It slowly warmed up his body again instead of experiencing the shock of a sudden change of temperature.

Within days Armando was on his feet, though he was still confused and forgetful. Doctors feared he might have suffered permanent brain damage, but gradually his thinking cleared. Reports of the stowaway had made international news, and he received letters of support from around the world. Cuban authorities demanded his return, though, and Armando was fearful that he would be sent back to Cuba where he most certainly would be jailed. Instead, his uncle invited Armando to join him in New Jersey.

DID YOU KNOW?

In cold temperatures the brain and body start to shut down. Some types of surgery use the process in a procedure called "induced hypothermia." It protects and preserves the brain and other organs during some types

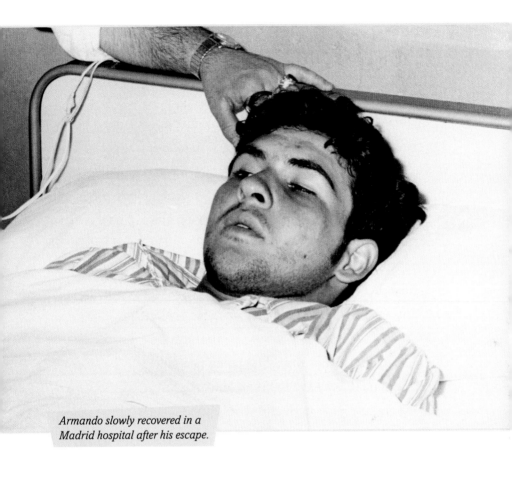
Armando slowly recovered in a Madrid hospital after his escape.

Two months later Armando was crossing the Atlantic on another airplane. This time he was safe, warm, comfortable, and conscious—and looking forward to a new life in the United States. "There was no future [in Cuba] at all for me," he told reporters in Spanish after he landed in New York. "I was looking for a new world and a new future." He had to fly right to the edge of death to reach it.

THE PLANE THAT COULDN'T STEER
UNITED FLIGHT 232

On July 19, 1989, everything was on schedule as United Flight 232 cruised along at 37,000 feet (11,300 m) above Iowa. The time was about 3:15 p.m., and the passenger jet was more than an hour into its flight from Denver to Chicago. The weather was good, and the flight attendants had just finished serving lunch. The three crew members in the cockpit—Captain Alfred Haynes, First Officer William Records, and Second Officer Dudley Dvorak—had the jet on autopilot. There was little to do until they prepared for landing near Chicago. Haynes was enjoying a cup of coffee.

BAM! An explosion sent a shudder through the DC-10. Captain Haynes thought a bomb had gone off. The aircraft lurched to the right, then started climbing sharply. First Officer Records immediately turned off the autopilot and took manual control of the jet. However, the plane would not respond to anything he tried. "Al, I can't control the airplane," Records told Haynes. The big jet was rolling slowly to the right, threatening to flip over and go into an uncontrolled dive.

The pilots had no idea what had happened, but they had only seconds to react. If they made a wrong move, the jet and its 296 passengers and crew would plummet to the ground. They had to regain some control of the plane quickly or they would all be dead. Their first guess was that one of the DC-10's three engines had failed.

Instinctively, Haynes reached for the throttles that controlled power to the engines, much like the gas pedal in a car. On instinct, he reduced power to engine one while ramming full power into engine three.

The desperation move worked. The right wing slowly came up until they were flying level again. They scanned their instruments, looking for some clue as to what had happened and what they could do about it. They discovered that the number-two engine—the one that ran through the tail section—was no longer operational. Engines one and three on the wings were undamaged.

United Flight 232 was quickly losing altitude as it flew toward Sioux City, Iowa.

Dvorak, seated behind Records, soon spotted a more frightening malfunction that filled him with alarm. The pressure in all three of the plane's hydraulic systems was dropping rapidly to zero. The news stunned Haynes and Records. In all their training, they had never heard of such a technical failure in a passenger jet.

Hydraulics is an amazing technology used in engineering and other sciences. It transfers mechanical power using pressurized fluid through tubes and pipes. In modern aircraft, hydraulics makes it possible for a pilot to sit in the cockpit and control the aircraft's landing gear, large flaps in the wings and tail, and other equipment with the flick of a switch or turn of a knob.

Somehow, all three hydraulic systems of the aircraft had been ruptured. Without hydraulics, the jet lacked almost any means to steer—left or right, up or down. It could not use its wing flaps to slow its speed. Not even the brakes on the landing gear would work. Almost all of the DC-10's control systems were useless, except the throttles controlling engine power.

BACK IN THE CABIN

The crew in the cockpit knew they were in serious trouble. However, they didn't want to panic the passengers. Second Officer Dvorak switched on the intercom. He announced that one engine had failed but they could still make it to Chicago with the other two. Dvorak then rang the flight attendants' station and spoke to Jan Brown, the head flight attendant. He asked her to come to the cockpit.

Brown knew the news had to be bad but kept a calm and professional demeanor as she walked to the front of the plane. When Haynes told her they had lost all hydraulics, her breath caught in her throat. She was sure she was going to die. Brown

United 232 crew recounted their ordeal on the 25th anniversary of the crash.

returned to the cabin and quietly informed the other flight attendants of the dire situation.

Dennis Fitch was one of the passengers in first class. He was an off-duty DC-10 training check airman for United Airlines. It was his job to train DC-10 pilots and to prepare them for every form of emergency. He knew the plane would be fine flying on just two engines. However, he had the sense that something more serious was going on. He stopped one of the passing flight attendants, Virginia Jane Murray. In a whisper, so as not to alarm the other passengers, she told him about the total failure of the hydraulic systems.

Scorched ground showed the path of the crash across the runways.

The news stunned Fitch. "That's impossible," he replied. "It can't happen." He had never heard of an airliner flying without functioning hydraulics, and he also knew that the jet could not land safely without those systems. He asked Murray to inform the captain that a trainer was aboard and that he was willing to help, if needed. Murray relayed the message, and Fitch soon joined the team in the cockpit.

Meanwhile, Dvorak had been communicating with flight controllers on the ground. The plane was redirected to Iowa's Sioux City Gateway Airport, about 70 miles (110 km) from their current position. But even if they could make it there, no one knew how they could possibly land the crippled aircraft.

The aircraft was losing altitude quickly—at about a rate of 500 feet (150 m) per minute. At the same time, it was making a slow turn to the right. Without control of the flaps, the nose repeatedly dipped, then rose, like a dolphin diving in and out of the water. All the while, though, the jet was spiraling downward. Haynes remained calm, but he knew the truth of the situation. At one point he radioed air traffic control: "Whatever you do, keep us away from the city." If they were going to crash and explode, he didn't want it to be in the heart of downtown Sioux City, home to more than 80,000 people.

As a team, the crew in the cockpit was figuring out how to use the two remaining engines on the wings to give them some control. Leaning between the pilot and copilot seats, Fitch was put in charge of the throttle controls. Under the direction of Haynes, he adjusted the thrust to the engines. They were able to keep the plane level with some control over direction.

"BRACE! BRACE! BRACE!"

Captain Haynes could no longer avoid telling the passengers the truth of what they were facing. About 20 minutes after the explosion, he informed them they were going to have to make an emergency landing in Sioux City. Haynes said he would warn them by saying the word "brace" three times before impact. Passengers gasped and cried out as they realized the danger they were in. Brown and the other flight attendants did their best to calm them. They made sure everyone had their seat belts fastened. Passengers were instructed about the brace position: leaning forward with feet flat on the floor.

In the cockpit, Fitch was using the throttles to turn the DC-10 to the left. The pilots succeeded in lining up the jet with an abandoned runway of the Sioux City airport. They were coming in at an altitude that gave them a chance to reach it. They released excess jet fuel from the plane's tanks to lessen any explosion and fire on impact. Fitch lowered the landing gear by hand, using mechanical handles under the cockpit.

On the ground, fire trucks and other rescue vehicles were rushing into position, their crews ready to jump into action. The hospital was notified to add staff to help possible survivors. "You're cleared to land on any runway," air traffic control told the incoming jet.

Federal investigators inspected one of the burned engines at the crash site.

"You want to be particular and make it a runway, huh?" Haynes joked. The humor broke some of the tension in the cockpit and control tower.

The flight crew had done a remarkable job of maneuvering the stricken aircraft without any of the usual controls. However, their speed was one factor over which they had little control. Without working wing flaps, they could not slow down as much as they needed to. They were traveling at about 250 miles (400 km) per hour, twice the normal speed for a safe landing. They were also dropping way too fast—about 1,800 feet (550 m) per minute—six times faster than a normal landing. There was nothing they could do about it. There was no way the landing gear could withstand that kind of shock, though it might absorb some of the force. The "emergency landing" would be a crash, and they knew it.

Still, they all tried their best to beat the odds. The DC-10 was coming in level and was on course for the old runway. The plane was going to smack into the ground, but the runway was surrounded by open farm fields. There was room for the jet to skid without hitting anything besides corn. The doomed flight seemed on the verge of a miracle.

With seconds to go before reaching the ground, the dreaded command came over the intercom: "Brace! Brace! Brace!"

Then Fitch made one last adjustment to the throttles. But the engines did not respond properly. At just 100 feet (30 m) in the air, the plane jerked sharply to the right. In the flight recordings, someone can be heard saying, "Left throttle, left, left, left …" but it was too late. The right wing and right landing gear ripped into the runway traveling more than 250 miles (400 km) per hour.

The people in the control tower watched as their worst fears came true. The aircraft broke apart as soon as it hit the ground, pieces flying in every direction. The tail and rear engine tore off. The loss of that weight in the back of the aircraft caused the nose to pitch forward. The engine on the left wing was still running at full power and the thrust twisted the plane to the right. It cartwheeled, then bounced once on its nose. The cockpit tore away. Leaking fuel erupted into a fireball, creating a huge cloud of black smoke. The center section of the plane split open. Some passengers, still strapped in their seats, were catapulted from the wreckage. Pieces of the plane skidded down the runway, then slid off to the right. What was left of the fuselage turned over and landed on its top.

Ambulances and fire trucks raced toward the smoking wreckage after it came to a stop. The entire area was covered with debris. At first the controllers and others at the airport were sure no one could have survived the crash. Rescue workers saw dozens of bodies lying in the grass around the runway. Then, amazingly, some of them sat up. Some of them stood. Some people emerged from the center section of the plane that had not been torn open. Passengers helped each other as they stumbled away from the wreckage and into the arms of first responders. After about a half hour, rescue workers found the crushed and almost unrecognizable cockpit containing Haynes, Records, Dvorak, and Fitch. Incredibly, all four of them were alive, though they had been knocked unconscious. They were rushed to the hospital to treat their injuries, and all four survived.

Of the 296 people on board, 185 survived. A few passengers walked away without injuries, but 171 people had serious injuries including burns and broken bones. A month later one

Cranes lifted the tail section of the plane onto a truck during the cleanup process.

survivor died of injuries sustained in the crash. One hundred twelve passengers were killed, including 11 children. Experts who studied the crash, though, were astonished so many had lived. Most of the survivors had been seated in the section in front of the wings.

Investigators praised the crew for controlling the plane as much as they did. After the crash, the quick arrival of firefighters and other emergency services also saved lives. Survivors included all but one of the crew members. Flight attendant Rene LeBeau was killed in the crash. The rest of the crew all eventually returned to flight duty.

AFTERMATH

As with all air crashes in the United States, the National Transportation Safety Board (NTSB) investigated. They collected the shattered pieces of United Flight 232 and inspected them closely, looking for clues as to what caused the accident. They studied the flight data recorder, also known as the "black box." Every commercial jet has a black box that records all information about the aircraft's operation, including all flight data, such as speed and altitude, the conversation and actions in the cockpit, and radio communications.

In the end, investigators found the cause of the crash in what was left of engine two. A tiny crack in one of its fans had caused it to disintegrate. As the fan flew apart, pieces ripped through the plane's three hydraulic systems, causing all the hydraulic fluid to drain out. After the findings, the U.S. Federal Aviation Administration (FAA) ordered a review of these fans in all DC-10 engines. They were inspected and replaced.

Remembering the crash years afterward, Captain Haynes told a newspaper, "We were too busy [to be scared]. You must maintain your composure in the airplane, or you will die. You learn that from your first day of flying."

The crash of United Flight 232 was a terrible disaster. However, the crew's efforts saved many lives. They used quick thinking, steady hands, and teamwork to bring a badly damaged aircraft back to Earth. The survivors still gather to mark that day and to remember those who did not survive.

Survivors and Sioux City community members gathered for a memorial 25 years after the crash.

DID YOU KNOW?

Every commercial aircraft is equipped with a "black box." Capable of withstanding tremendous force, these flight data recorders offer vital clues about the causes of a crash. In reality, black boxes are bright orange to make them more visible, and there are two aboard the aircraft, each recording a different set of data. They send out radio signals to make them easier to find in the event of a crash.

"LA MIRACULÉE"
YEMENIA FLIGHT 626

Bahia Bakari, 13, was in a window seat of an Airbus A310 on its way to Comoros, an island off East Africa. As the aircraft descended toward the airport, the cabin lights flickered and the plane shuddered and shook. Bahia noticed that one of the flight attendants seemed nervous, even as she tried to reassure everyone that the turbulence was normal. The plane's 142 passengers were asked to put on their seat belts. Bahia's mother, Aziza Aboudou, smiled and ran a hand across Bahia's hair to comfort her.

A beach on Comoros features the unique terrain and landscape of the island.

Bahia pressed her face against the window to look out, hoping she might see city lights in the night. It was after midnight and they were nearing their destination.

Suddenly there was a loud whistling in the cabin. Bahia heard explosions and the crunch of metal. She felt tremendous pressure push on her from all sides. The next thing she knew, her mother was no longer beside her and she was no longer in the aircraft. In fact, the aircraft was gone.

FLYING TO FAMILY

Bahia and her mother had waved goodbye to Bahia's father at the airport in Paris, France. Summer vacation had begun, and the teenager was looking forward to a break from school and a chance to visit family in Comoros.

The country of Comoros consists of three main islands. They lie near Africa's eastern coastline and the large island country of Madagascar. Before gaining independence in 1975, Comoros had been a colony of France. For some 175 years, it was controlled by the French government in Paris. Many of its people, including Bahia's parents, had emigrated to France in search of better opportunities. Now Bahia was going to Comoros to visit her grandmother and other relatives who still lived there.

Bahia and her mother's trip began by flying from Paris to the French city of Marseille to pick up more passengers. They then continued on to Sana'a, Yemen, on the Arabian Peninsula. There, on June 29, 2009, they boarded Yemenia Flight 626, an Airbus A310 passenger jet.

CONGO

Dodoma

TANZANIA

Dar es Salaam

SEYCHELLES

Lubumbashi

Moroni

MALAWI

Lilongwe

COMOROS

Antsiranana

ZAMBIA

Lusaka

Harare

MOZAMBIQUE

Tomasina

ZIMBABWE

Antananarivo

Beira

MADAGASCAR

TSWANA

Fianarantsoa

one

Tulear

Pretoria

Maputo

Tolanaro

annesburg

Mbabane

SWAZILAND

LESOTHO

Maseru

'H

Durban

:A

INDIAN OCEAN

Port Elizabeth

Comoros is an island country formed
by volcanic eruptions off the coast of
East Africa.

The aircraft took off and began its southward journey. It landed briefly in the country of Djibouti, then flew over the Horn of Africa. The next stop was to be Moroni, the capital of Comoros and Bahia and her mother's final destination.

The flight was scheduled to arrive at Moroni's Prince Said Ibrahim International Airport. It is known as a tricky place to land. Weather conditions there are unpredictable, including strong winds and ocean storms. The hills around the airport also create difficulties for pilots. Some crews receive special training before flying there. According to the International Federation of Air Line Pilots Association, some airlines consider Moroni a "daytime-only airport." In other words, attempting to land there with the added challenge of darkness makes some airlines consider it unsafe for nighttime landings.

Flight 626, though, was scheduled to arrive after midnight. It seems the flight crew struggled with the approach and tried to circle around for another try. They never made it.

Shortly before 1:30 a.m. local time, the jet plunged into the Indian Ocean and was torn apart.

THE LONGEST NIGHT

Bahia had no idea what had happened. In an instant, she went from sitting inside the airplane to struggling underwater. She rose to the surface, gasping for air. Her mouth was raw from salt water and jet fuel from the aircraft's ruptured fuel tanks. She tried to get her bearings and figure out where she was and how she had gotten there. Had she leaned too hard against the window and fallen out of the aircraft? She worried that her mother would be angry with her for being so careless.

All Bahia knew was that she was in the ocean in the dark of night. She hurt all over, especially her legs, shoulder, and the left side of her face. She was not a strong swimmer and had no life vest. She was also weighed down by her soggy clothes and shoes.

Bahia spotted four pieces of debris floating not too far away. She fought her way toward the largest chunk, then attempted to climb onto it like a life raft. However, the piece of wreckage flipped over when she tried to crawl on top of it. All she could do was hold on to it, laying her upper body on its surface with her legs hanging down in the water. In the distance, she thought she heard women's voices calling for help. They faded and soon fell silent. She was all alone.

Hour after long hour passed in the night, the teenage girl clinging to the piece of debris. The sea was rough, and the cool water was sapping away her body heat. She soon lost all feeling in her legs as they hung in the water. Waves of nearly 20 feet (6 m) rose and fell around her. Exhausted, Bahia closed her eyes and tried to rest, her mind somewhere between waking and dozing. Finally, the sky began to grow brighter. Morning came. She was terribly thirsty.

As the sun rose, Bahia scanned the horizon as best she could. She spotted green hills of land in the distance and gave a yelp of joy. Land! She tried to paddle toward it. The ocean current, though, was far too strong. It was dragging her northward, away from the islands of Comoros. The green hills receded, then sank below the horizon.

At one point Bahia thought she heard aircraft overhead. She felt a surge of hope that rescuers were out searching for her. Still, there was nothing she could do but hang on, wait, and hope. No amount of shouting or waving would do any good across the vast ocean.

This is a Yemenia Airbus A310, similar to the one Bahia and her mother flew.

DID YOU KNOW?

Since 1970 there have been about 30 large plane crashes in which all but one passenger were killed. Seven of these sole-survivor crashes happened on or near the African continent.

The piece of wreckage that served as a life preserver had a window. Now that there was light, she looked through it and down into the water. She wished she hadn't. She spied dark shapes moving beneath her, filling her with even more fear. What could they be? Fish? Sharks? Bahia was terrified and began losing hope of being saved. The last bits of strength were draining away from her arms and upper body. She did not know how much longer she could hang on, and she was growing more and more confused. It would be so easy to give up.

But then Bahia glanced up and couldn't believe what she saw. A fishing boat was plowing toward her over the big waves. Comoros does not have its own navy or coast guard. Officials, though, had alerted fishing crews and the crews of other vessels about the downed jet. A Comoros-based French search plane and dozens of boats had fanned out in search of survivors.

Bahia tried to shout to get the boat's attention, though its crew had already seen her. In desperation, she let go of the hunk of wreckage that had kept her afloat and tried to swim toward her rescuers. The crew of the small boat were astonished when they spotted the girl struggling toward them. The waves overwhelmed her. The fishermen threw her a float, but Bahia was too weak to hold on to it. Then another big wave rolled over her, and she disappeared beneath the water.

One of the fishermen, Libouna Maturaffe Soulemane, realized the girl was floundering. He bravely jumped from the bow into the treacherous waves and battled his way to Bahia. He clutched her and helped her to the boat, where other crew

Search parties scoured the area off the coast of Comoros looking for survivors.

members pulled her from the water. "When I saw the girl, I was not afraid to dive in," Soulemane told reporters afterward. "She was calm. . . . She knew what she was doing. . . . The girl is very courageous."

Bahia was exhausted after some 13 hours in the water, but now she was safe. Her rescuers wrapped Bahia in blankets. They served her warm drinks with sugar to help bring up her body temperature and give her some strength. They pointed the bow of their boat toward land. At about 7:25 p.m. Bahia was brought ashore at Moroni.

In 2010 Bahia posed with the book she wrote about her experience.

Bahia BAKARI

Moi Bahia, la miraculée

Elle a 13 ans. Elle est la seule rescapée du crash du vol des Comores. Elle raconte Un récit bouleversant

SOLE SURVIVOR

An international team of air safety experts launched an investigation into the crash. They pinned the cause on pilot error. It seems the pilot miscalculated the approach to the runway at Moroni and aborted the first attempt to land. The aircraft tried to circle around for another try. However, the flight crew made a series of mistakes that caused the engines to stall. They could not regain control or get the engines back online. The aircraft slammed into the water about 9 miles (14 km) north of Moroni.

A month later the French navy recovered the flight recorders from the bottom of the sea. Data from them confirmed that mistakes by the pilot and copilot were responsible for the crash. Strong winds and a lack of training also contributed to the disaster.

Bahia Bakari woke up in a hospital in Moroni the day after her rescue. She had cuts and bruises on her face and body. Her collarbone and pelvis were broken. The first thing she asked about was her mother. Where was she? At first, an uncle told Bahia that her mother was in the next room. He did not want to cause his niece any more suffering. Later, though, a member of the hospital staff told Bahia the truth. Rescuers had not found Bahia's mother and she had likely perished. Her body was one of 84 that were later recovered.

Bahia was the sole survivor of the crash of Yemenia Flight 626. Everyone else aboard—152 passengers and crew—was killed. Bahia spent three weeks in the hospital in Moroni, healing and regaining her strength. Her father flew down to join her. French officials then flew them on a special jet back to Paris, where Bahia continued her recovery.

She had survived not only a catastrophic airplane crash but also being lost in the vastness of the Indian Ocean. The following year Bahia shared the tale of her terrifying ordeal in the book *Moi Bahia, La Miraculée—I Am Bahia, the Miracle Girl.*

DID YOU KNOW?

Not surprisingly, people in plane crashes experience high levels of stress and terror. Survivors often have flashbacks and nightmares about the crash afterward. Many receive treatment for post-traumatic stress and trauma to help

MIRACLE ON THE HUDSON
US AIRWAYS FLIGHT 1549

With more than 40 years of flying experience, Captain Chesley Sullenberger, 57, was a steady hand in the cockpit. January 15, 2009, was just another day on the job he loved as he readied his plane and crew on US Airways Flight 1549. Captain Sullenberger was as prepared as anyone could be for a crisis. He didn't know that today would be the day he'd need to draw on every bit of that preparation to save the lives of 155 people.

Growing up in Texas, Sullenberger had been an honor student at Denison High School. He graduated first in his class. At age 16 he had learned to fly at a small airstrip near his home and fell in love with flying. He was accepted into the United States Air Force Academy, the demanding training ground for officers in the U.S. Air Force (USAF). Graduating in 1973, he was named the Outstanding Cadet in Airmanship, marking him as an elite pilot. He served in the USAF for seven years, flying fighter jets and becoming a flight leader and trainer.

After leaving the Air Force in 1980, he became a commercial pilot, eventually joining US Airways. He was certified to fly almost anything with wings, including gliders. He also had been called on to investigate air crashes to figure out what had gone wrong in hopes of avoiding similar disasters in the future.

By 2009 Sullenberger had logged more than 20,000 hours in the air. He was a top expert in what aircraft could and could not do.

Captain Sullenberger (right) and Flight 1549 First Officer Jeff
Skiles (left) both learned to fly at age 16. In 2009 they became
co-chairs of the Experimental Aircraft Association's Young Eagles
program, which aims to get young people interested in aviation.

The January 15 flight was leaving from New York City's LaGuardia Airport, located in the borough of Queens in New York City. It is a small but busy airport that juts out into the East River. Pilots have compared LaGuardia—with water on three sides—to landing on and taking off from an aircraft carrier.

The 155 people aboard the Airbus A320 that day included three flight attendants, First Officer Jeffrey B. Skiles, and "Sully," as Sullenberger was known. They were bound for Charlotte, North Carolina. The aircraft would then continue across the continent to Seattle, Washington.

WHAT A VIEW

Just before 3:25 p.m. the flight was cleared for takeoff. Its twin engines roared as the plane raced down the runway. The acceleration pushed everyone back in their seats. The plane's wheels left the ground and the plane began climbing. "What a view of the Hudson today," Sullenberger remarked to Skiles, looking down on the river that runs along the west side of Manhattan.

Thirty seconds into their climb, though, Sullenberger exclaimed, "Birds!" The aircraft had flown through a flock of Canada geese, striking the large birds at 2,818 feet (859 m). Aircraft-bird collisions are relatively common. Jets and their engines are built to withstand most bird strikes and keep functioning.

Not this time. The geese slammed against the cockpit windows. Back in the cabin, passengers and crew heard the impacts as the geese hit the fuselage, wings, and engines. One of the engines suddenly spouted flames. Some passengers cried out.

In the cockpit Sullenberger and Skiles realized the bird strike had disabled both engines. The captain grabbed the controls while the first officer tried to restart the engines.

Sullenberger instantly radioed air traffic control with a Mayday—the international distress signal. "We've lost thrust on both engines. We're turning back towards LaGuardia," he said.

Air traffic controller Patrick Harten acknowledged the Mayday. Harten directed LaGuardia to clear the area for an emergency landing. He told the flight crew to try for Runway 13.

Almost immediately, though, Captain Sullenberger knew they would never make it back to the airport. He responded with two words: "We're unable."

US Airways Flight 1549 was gliding only 3,000 (914 m) feet above New York City. Flying without engine power, the plane had nothing to keep it in the air. It would come down—and fast. And below them was a city of millions.

DID YOU KNOW?

"Mayday" is the international term used by ships and aircraft when calling for help. It comes from the French word *m'aider,* which means "help me." Mayday was made the world's official distress signal in 1948.

HIGH STAKES

With more than 8.5 million residents, New York City is the most populated city in the United States. Including the surrounding suburbs and cities, the urban area is home to more than 20 million people.

Not surprisingly, the New York City region is also one of the busiest for air travel in the world. It is served by three major airports—LaGuardia and John F. Kennedy International, both in Queens, and Newark Liberty International in New Jersey. About 4,000 flights come into and out of these three air hubs every day. In 2008, the year before Flight 1549, about 107 million air passengers passed through them. (By 2017 that figure had risen to 132 million passengers.)

Now a large passenger jet was at risk of crashing into this densely populated area, and Sullenberger needed to come up with a plan—fast.

An illustration portrays the moment the plane hit the geese, causing severe damage to the engines.

DITCHING

After striking the flock of geese, Captain Sullenberger and First Officer Skiles were unable to restart the engines. For all practical purposes, the Airbus A320 was now a 75-ton glider. The plane continued its flight path over the northern section of New York City. However, it was losing altitude. The clock was ticking on how long they could stay airborne.

Sullenberger asked air controllers for landing options in New Jersey, across the Hudson River. He was given permission to try for Teterboro Airport. The two pilots scanned their instruments and, within moments, realized the chances of making it there were slim. Sullenberger didn't hesitate. "We can't do it," he said. "We're gonna be in the Hudson."

A series of quick calculations ran through Sullenberger's head. He and Skiles needed to keep the plane aloft for as long as possible. They needed to put it down in a place that increased the chances of keeping the plane from breaking up on impact. Sullenberger also wanted a location where rescuers could reach the plane as fast as possible. The aircraft was equipped with life vests, life rafts, and other gear and equipment to help the passengers and crew survive a water landing. In a matter of moments, Sullenberger's experience calculated that landing on the calm waters of the Hudson River was everyone's best chance of survival.

At 3:28 p.m.—less than three minutes after the bird strike—Sullenberger began a southward turn. He was lining up to ditch the plane in the Hudson River.

The jet cleared the 604-foot (184-m) George Washington Bridge by a mere 900 feet (274 m). Without the familiar roar and whine of the engines, the powerless aircraft was strangely silent. It was soon clear to everyone in the cabin that the aircraft was going down. The flight attendants calmly but urgently told the passengers to find the life vests under their seats and put them on. Passengers say the cabin was filled with the sounds of people praying.

Sullenberger and Skiles had no time to explain the situation to the passengers. Finally, Sullenberger turned on the intercom and gave the order no airline pilot ever wants to give. "This is your captain. Brace for impact." Passengers bent over in their seats. The flight attendants began a chant over the loudspeakers to help passengers stay focused on what they needed to do: "Brace. Brace. Heads down. Stay down."

Meanwhile, air traffic controllers on the ground were alerting the Coast Guard. They asked Coast Guard crews to warn vessels away from that area of the Hudson River and prepare for rescue operations.

Wheels up, the aircraft came soaring down toward the river at about 140 miles (225 km) per hour. It was important to keep both wings level as the plane's underbelly touched water. If one wing hit the water first, the Airbus would likely cartwheel and be ripped apart.

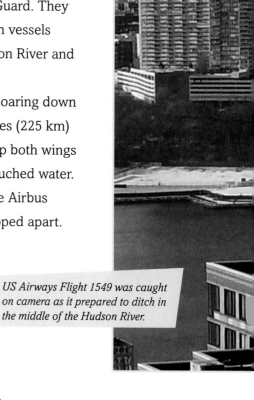

US Airways Flight 1549 was caught on camera as it prepared to ditch in the middle of the Hudson River.

At 3:31 p.m. everyone aboard felt the rough smack of a hard landing. The force jerked them in their seats. Some people struck their heads against the seat backs in front of them. The aircraft then glided to a quick stop on the water's surface. The fuselage was still intact, though one engine had broken off.

Investigators would later say Sullenberger could not have done the water landing in a better location. That part of the Hudson is about 4,000 feet (1,220 m) wide—the equivalent of more than 13 football fields end to end. Sullenberger also had ditched the plane in a stretch of river where boat crews were ready to help.

The aircraft and those aboard were still not out of danger, however. Sullenberger emerged from the cockpit ordering a quick evacuation. There was still the risk of a fire or explosion, and there was no telling how long they had before the aircraft sank in the river. The water landing had knocked open cargo doors and punched a hole in the plane's underbelly. In a panic, one passenger also had opened a rear exit door that could not be closed again. Now water was rushing into the cabin, rising up to the waists of some passengers.

The crew directed passengers to four emergency exits over the wings. Some passengers had put on life vests; others had not. Emergency slides that also serve as life rafts were inflated on both sides of the plane. Passengers climbed out, some getting into the waterlogged rafts while others stood on the wings. A few people panicked and jumped into the freezing water to swim away from the aircraft. Captain Sullenberger twice inspected the inside of his plane to make sure everyone was safely out. He was the last person to exit. The passengers shivered as they waited for rescue. The January temperature outside was just 19°F (-7°C). Within minutes, though, nine vessels arrived alongside the aircraft as the river current carried it down the Hudson. Rescuers began taking passengers off the waterlogged plane and plucking others from the water. The passengers and crew were transported to shore for treatment, mostly for exposure to the cold. Only five people suffered serious injuries, and all 155 on the plane survived.

From takeoff to the last rescue, the entire "Miracle on the Hudson" had taken 30 minutes.

HONORS AND INVESTIGATION

People around the United States, and the world, saw footage of the emergency landing and rescue efforts. The National Transportation Safety Board called it "the most successful ditching in aviation history."

Captain Sullenberger and First Officer Skiles were hailed for their cool heads and steely nerves. They and the flight attendants were honored time and again for their heroism. The crews of the rescue boats and other first responders were also praised for their quick work in getting passengers to safety.

All 155 passengers and crew were able to exit the plane and wait for rescue.

The engine of US Airways Flight 1549 was lifted from the Hudson River a week after the crash.

The Airbus 320 was pulled from the Hudson River a few days later. Investigators disassembled its twin engines and found feathers and other evidence of the bird strike. While jet engines are designed to withstand impacts with most birds, the large size of the Canada geese in this case caused too much damage for the engines to continue to function.

Captain Chesley Sullenberger retired a little more than a year later. First Officer Skiles joined him in the cockpit for his last professional flight. A handful of passengers from Flight 1549 came to offer another round of thanks.

Later, Sullenberger reflected on what made the Miracle on the Hudson possible. "One way of looking at this might be that for 42 years, I've been making small, regular deposits in this bank of experience, education, and training," he said in an interview. "And on January 15, [2009], the balance was sufficient so that I could make a very large withdrawal."

DID YOU KNOW?

The Airbus A320 made famous by the Miracle on the Hudson is now a museum piece. You can visit the reconstructed aircraft at the Carolinas Aviation Museum in Charlotte, North Carolina.

GLOSSARY

bush pilot—a pilot who flies in remote, unsettled areas

cockpit—the space in the front of the plane where the pilot controls the aircraft

disintegrate—to break up

ditch—to land a plane on water in an emergency landing

embargo—a restriction on trade or commerce

fuselage—the central body structure of an aircraft

hydraulics—technology that uses pressurized fluid to transfer mechanical force

hypothermia—a life-threatening condition that occurs when a person's body temperature falls several degrees below normal

Mayday—an international distress call used by aircraft and ships

NTSB—National Transportation Safety Board; government agency that investigates plane crashes

retract—to pull back

turbulence—air disturbance during flight

READ MORE

Burgan, Michael. *The Hindenburg in Flames: How a Photograph Marked the End of the Airship.* North Mankato, MN: Capstone Press, 2019.

Otfinoski, Steven. *Captain Sully's River Landing: The Hudson Hero of Flight 1549.* North Mankato, MN: Capstone Press, 2019.

Surges, Carol S. *The Science of a Plane Crash.* Ann Arbor, MI: Cherry Lake Publishing, 2014.

INTERNET SITES

Aviation for Kids
http://www.aviation-for-kids.com

National Transportation Safety Board: What does the NTSB do, anyway?
https://www.ntsb.gov/news/speeches/rsumwalt/
Documents/sumwalt_20161212.pdf

Popular Mechanics: How Plane Crashes Help Improve Safety
https://www.popularmechanics.com/flight/g73/12-airplane-crashes-that-changed-aviation/

SOURCE NOTES

p. 8, "This is pretty bad…" Kyle Hopkins, "Plane Crash Survivors in the Alaskan Wilderness," *Reader's Digest*, January 2014, https://www.rd.com/true-stories/survival/plane-crash-survivors-alaskan-wilderness/ Accessed on March 14, 2019.

p. 8, "Pull up!…" Kyle Hopkins, "After the Crash: Family Tells of 15-hour Fight for Survival," *Anchorage Daily News*, May 11, 2013, https://www.adn.com/anchorage/article/after-crash-family-tells-15-hour-fight-survival/2013/05/12/ Accessed on February 26, 2019.

p. 12, "These things we do…" Alli Harvey, "Alaskans' Safety Net: The Crack 212th Rescue Squadron," *Anchorage Daily News*, December 2, 2017, https://www.adn.com/alaska-life/we-alaskans/2017/03/12/alaskans-safety-net-the-crack-212th-rescue-squadron/ Accessed on March 14, 2019.

p. 22, "Impossible! Impossible!…" Armando Socarrás Ramirez. "I Escaped From Cuba in the Wheels of a DC-8," *Reader's Digest*, January 1970, https://www.rd.com/true-stories/survival/escape-from-cuba-dc-8/ Accessed on February 26, 2019.

p. 25, "There was no future…" Edward E. Leslie. *Desperate Journeys, Abandoned Souls: True Stories of Castaways and Other Survivors*. New York: Houghton Mifflin Company, 1998, p. 471.

p. 26, "Al, I can't control the airplane…" Lawrence Gonzalez, "The Crash of United Flight 232," *Popular Mechanics*, July 18, 2017, https://www.popularmechanics.com/flight/a10478/the-final-flight-of-united-232-16755928/ Accessed on February 26, 2019.

p. 30, "That's impossible…" Gabe Andino, "United Flight 232: Surviving the Unthinkable," NYC Aviation, July 18, 2014, http://www.nycaviation.com/2014/07/disaster-miracle-united-flight-232/34639 Accessed on February 26, 2019.

p. 31, "Whatever you do…" "19 July 1989—United 232," Cockpit Voice Recorder Database, https://www.tailstrike.com/190789.htm Accessed on February 26, 2019.

p. 32, "You're cleared to land…" "United Flight 232: Surviving the Unthinkable."

p. 33, "You want to be particular…" Ibid.

p. 33, "Left throttle…" "Humor, Drama Mixed Aboard Doomed Jet," *Chicago Tribune,* September 19, 1989, https://www.chicagotribune.com/news/ct-xpm-1989-09-19-8901140311-story.html Accessed on February 26, 2019.

p. 36, "We were too busy…" Dominic Gates, "20 Years Ago, Pilot's Heroic Efforts Saved 185 People as Plane Crashed," *The Seattle Times*, July 19, 2009, https://www.seattletimes.com/seattle-news/20-years-ago-pilots-heroic-efforts-saved-185-people-as-plane-crashed/ Accessed on February 26, 2019.

p. 41, "daytime-only airport" "'Miracle' Crash Girl Survived 13 Hours at Sea," NBCNews.com, July 2, 2009, http://www.nbcnews.com/id/31678931/ns/world_news-africa/t/miracle-crash-girl-survived-hours-sea/#.XHWMlC2ZN25 Accessed on February 26, 2019.

p. 45, "When I saw the girl…" Jason Burke, "'When I Saw the Girl, I Wasn't Afraid to Dive In,'" *The Guardian*, July 5, 2009, https://www.theguardian.com/world/2009/jul/05/yemenia-plane-crash-girl-rescue Accessed on February 26, 2019.

p. 50, "What a view of the Hudson today…" Katherine Santiago, "'Miracle on the Hudson' US Airways Flight 1549 Transcript Released," NJ.com, June 9, 2009, https://www.nj.com/news/index.ssf/2009/06/cockpit_radio_communication_tr.html Accessed on February 26, 2019.

p. 50, "Birds!…" McClatchy, "Hero Pilot 'Sully' Sullenberger Recalls 'Miracle on the Hudson' Landing 10 Years Later," Aviation Pros, January 15, 2019, https://www.aviationpros.com/aircraft/commercial-airline/news/12440485/hero-pilot-sully-sullenberger-recalls-miracle-on-the-hudson-landing-10-years-later Accessed March 14, 2019.

p. 51, "We've lost thrust…" "15 January 2009 — US Airways 1549," Cockpit Recorder Database, https://www.tailstrike.com/150109.htm Accessed March 14, 2019.

p. 51, "We're unable…" Ibid.

p. 53, "We can't do it…" Ibid.

p. 54, "This is your captain…" Ibid.

p. 54, "Brace. Brace. Heads down…" Georgia Debelius, "Passengers Recall Terrifying Experiences Onboard Hudson River Flight 1549 Behind New Hollywood Film Sully," *Metro*, November 28, 2016, https://metro.co.uk/2016/11/28/passengers-recall-terrifying-experiences-onboard-hudson-river-flight-1549-behind-new-hollywood-film-sully-6286805/ Accessed on February 26, 2019.

p. 57, "The most successful ditching…" Oliver Smith, "The Most Heroic Airline Pilots of All Time," *The Telegraph*, January 15, 2019, https://www.telegraph.co.uk/travel/lists/The-9-most-heroic-airline-pilots-of-all-time/ Accessed March 14, 2019.

p. 59, "One way of looking…" Sandy Smith, "NSC 2012: Captain Sullly Sullenberger Talks About the Miracle on the Hudson River," *EHS Today*, October 22, 2012, https://www.ehstoday.com/safety/nsc-2012-captain-sully-sullenberger-talks-about-miracle-hudson-river Accessed on February 26, 2019.

SELECT BIBLIOGRAPHY

Books

Bakari, Bahia. *Moi Bahia, La Miraculée*. Paris: De Noyelles, 2009.

Bovsun, Mara and Allan Zullo. *The Greatest Survivor Stories Never Told*. Kansas City, MO: Andrews McMeel Publishing, 2002.

Leslie, Edward E. *Desperate Journeys, Abandoned Souls: True Stories of Castaways and Other Survivors*. New York: Houghton Mifflin Company, 1998.

Websites and Articles

"19 July 1989—United 232," Cockpit Voice Recorder Database/Tailstrike.com, https://www.tailstrike.com/190789.htm Accessed on February 26, 2019.

"Fact Sheet—General Aviation Safety," Federal Aviation Administration, July 30, 2018, https://www.faa.gov/news/fact_sheets/news_story.cfm?newsId=21274 Accessed on February 26, 2019.

"The Medical Conundrum of Plane Stowaways," *BBC Magazine*, June 24, 2015, https://www.bbc.com/news/magazine-33222405 Accessed on February 26, 2019.

Adams, Eric, "Family of 4 Survives Bush Alaska Plane Crash that Killed 2 Others," *Anchorage Daily News*, August 15, 2011, https://www.adn.com/alaska-news/article/family-4-survives-bush-alaska-plane-crash-killed-2-others/2011/08/15/ Accessed on February 26, 2019.

Andino, Gabe, "United Flight 232: Surviving the Unthinkable," NYC Aviation, July 18, 2014, http://www.nycaviation.com/2014/07/disaster-miracle-united-flight-232/34639 Accessed on February 26, 2019.

Associated Press, "'Miracle' Crash Girl Survived 13 Hours at Sea," NBCNews.com, July 2, 2009, http://www.nbcnews.com/id/31678931/ns/world_news-africa/t/miracle-crash-girl-survived-hours-sea/#.XHWMlC2ZN25 Accessed on February 26, 2019.

Associated Press/Tom Maliti and Angela Charlton, "Teen Air-Crash Survivor 'Didn't Feel a Thing,'" *Time.com*, July 1, 2009, https://www.webcitation.org/5iPU1SkV4?url=http://www.time.com/time/world/article/0,8599,1908048,00.html Accessed on February 26, 2019.

Campbell, Matthew, "Airbus Crash Girl, Bahia Bakari, Tells Story of Miraculous Survival," *The Australian*, December 28, 2009, https://www.theaustralian.com.au/news/world/airbus-crash-girl-bahia-bakari-tells-story-of-miraculous-survival/news-story/5b5af19cd586404f663365af23c87dfa Accessed on February 26, 2019.

Case, Samantha et al., "Work-Related Nonfatal Injuries in Alaska's Aviation Industry, 2000–2013," U.S. National Library of Medicine National Institutes of Health, April 2018, https://www.ncbi.nlm.nih.gov/pmc/articles/PMC5875429/ Accessed on February 26, 2019.

Coburn, Davin, "Piper Pa-18 Super Cub: The Perfect Bush Plane," *Popular Mechanics*, May 13, 2011, https://www.popularmechanics.com/flight/how-to/a6657/piper-pa-18-super-cub-the-perfect-bush-plane/ Accessed on February 26, 2019.

Diebelius, Georgia, "Passengers Recall Terrifying Experiences Onboard Hudson River Flight 1549 Behind New Hollywood Film Sully," *Metro*, November 28, 2016, https://metro.co.uk/2016/11/28/passengers-recall-terrifying-experiences-onboard-hudson-river-flight-1549-behind-new-hollywood-film-sully-6286805/ Accessed on February 26, 2019.

Gonzalez, Lawrence, "The Crash of United Flight 232," *Popular Mechanics*, July 18, 2017, https://www.popularmechanics.com/flight/a10478/the-final-flight-of-united-232-16755928/ Accessed on February 26, 2019.

Hopkins, Kyle, "After the Crash: Family Tells of 15-hour Fight for Survival," *Anchorage Daily News*, May 11, 2013, https://www.adn.com/anchorage/article/after-crash-family-tells-15-hour-fight-survival/2013/05/12/ Accessed on February 26, 2019.

Hopkins, Kyle, "Plane Crash Survivors in the Alaskan Wilderness," *Reader's Digest*, January 2014, https://www.rd.com/true-stories/survival/plane-crash-survivors-alaskan-wilderness/3/ Accessed on March 14, 2019.

Hopkins, Kyle, and Tom Bell, "Plane Crash Survivors on the Mend in Maine," *PressHerald.com*, May 11, 2013, https://www.pressherald.com/2013/05/11/on-the-mend-in-maine_2013-05-12/ Accessed on February 26, 2019.

McClatchy, "Hero Pilot 'Sully' Sullenberger Recalls 'Miracle on the Hudson' Landing 10 Years Later," *Aviation Pros*, January 15, 2019, https://www.aviationpros.com/aircraft/commercial-airline/news/12440485/hero-pilot-sully-sullenberger-recalls-miracle-on-the-hudson-landing-10-years-later Accessed March 14, 2019.

Northedge, Charlotte, "The Only Ones: Escaping Near Death," *The Guardian*, September 4, 2010, https://www.theguardian.com/world/2010/sep/04/only-ones-sole-survivors-near-death Accessed on February 26, 2019.

Pi, Vanessa, "Hacía Mucho Frío y el Ruido Era Ensordecedor," *Publico*, July 7, 2015, https://www.publico.es/espana/hacia-mucho-frio-y-ruido.html Accessed on February 26, 2019.

Ramirez, Armando Socorrás, "I Escaped From Cuba in the Wheels of a DC-8," *Reader's Digest*, January 1970, https://www.rd.com/true-stories/survival/escape-from-cuba-dc-8/ Accessed on February 26, 2019.

Santiago, Katherine, "'Miracle on the Hudson' US Airways Flight 1549 Transcript Released," NJ.com, June 9, 2009, https://www.nj.com/news/index.ssf/2009/06/cockpit_radio_communication_tr.html Accessed on February 26, 2019.

Smith, Oliver, "The Most Heroic Airline Pilots of All Time," *The Telegraph*, January 15, 2019, https://www.telegraph.co.uk/travel/lists/The-9-most-heroic-airline-pilots-of-all-time/ Accessed March 14, 2019.

St. John, Allen, "What Went Right: Revisiting Captain 'Sully' Sullenberger and the Miracle on the Hudson," *Popular Mechanics*, January 15, 2019, https://www.popularmechanics.com/flight/a4137/sully-sullenberger-us-air-flight-1549-miracle-hudson/ Accessed on February 26, 2019.

INDEX

ABOUT THE AUTHOR

Sean McCollum was 19 before he nervously walked onto a passenger jet for the first time. Since then, he has spent a lot of time in the air, traveling to 65 countries on six continents. He is the author of more than 40 books and hundreds of magazine articles for young people. You can follow his misadventures at www.kidfreelance.com. Sean ALWAYS fastens his seat belt and locates the nearest emergency exit.